An Effective Self-Publishing Handbook

Step #1: Write Your eBook

Publishing is what you do after you've written a book. It has to come after the actual writing process, which sort of puts it on the back burner for any writer or author whose book is still a work in progress.

No matter what you write, you do have an audience and they will read your book if you put it out there and promote it effectively.

But ultimately, the quality of the book will have a direct effect on how successful it will be following publication. I doubt that any writer will disagree with stressing the importance of this step in the publishing process --- the writing is arguably the heart of everything when it comes to publishing your first book. This is the step that will likely take the most time, care, inspiration, editing, skill and talent.

If you plan on self-publishing your own book or ebook as a debut author, you'll certainly have your work cut out for you once your work is finished. But perhaps surprisingly, very little of that work will involve further writing. It focuses on and demands efforts in several different areas, but writing is not among the most important.

Being successful in self-publishing your own books requires an individual who is somewhat a jack of all trades, unless you have the money to shell out for professional services to take care of editing, cover design, printing and publicizing your book.

In order to avoid being labeled as vanity published, I think it's best to take on as much of the project as you can realistically commit to. This is just my personal opinion, but it makes sense to me for an independent author to be, well, just that --- truly independent.

4 Important Elements of the Writing Process

1. **Fitting writing into your daily life in a practical way.**
   - When do you find time to write?
   - How do you manage to write at least a little bit each day, without having to take significant time from other important aspects of your life?
   - What writing exercises do you make daily habits?

2. **Finding inspiration and topics for your writing.**
   - What do you write about?
   - What genre are you most comfortable with, fiction or non-fiction?
   - What do you readers want, and how can you deliver in a way that brings them back for your next book?
   - Who is your audience and what appeals to them?
   - Learn more here: <u>10 Effective Steps to Amazingly Inspirational Writing</u>

3. **Developing a long-term writing plan.**
    - Are you writing a memoir, or will this be your first book in a series of fiction novels?
    - How long do you want your first book to be, or is that important within your genre?
    - Who are your characters and how do you plan on developing them?
    - If you're writing non-fiction, how will your first book introduce the topics you are likely to write books about in the future?
    - What is your writing strategy for setting yourself apart from other writers in your genre?
    - Have you started brainstorming ideas for a title? Learn more here: <u>10 Questions to Ask Before Writing Your Book</u>

4. **Editing, proofreading and revising.**
    - If you're not hiring an editor, what is your plan for editing your book to look as professional as possible?
    - Have you read through your entire book to check for errors, typos or awkwardness in grammar?
    - Has anyone else read through it as well?
    - Have you spell checked the entire manuscript?
    - Have you removed words that are unnecessary and taken out parts that bog down the writing?
    - How often have you revisited the writing to make appropriate revisions?
    - Learn more here: <u>10 Proofreading Tips to Ensure Your Self-Published Works are Flawless</u>

Ideas for Your Fiction eBook

- Collection of short stories
- Fiction novel
- Fiction series
- Collection of poetry

Ideas for Your Non-Fiction eBook

- Collection of your most popular blog posts
- A how-to guide, tutorial or course
- A personal journal or memoir (<u>Journal Writing Tools and Resources</u>)
- Compilation of essays, research or opinion writing

Have a writing idea that's not quite long enough to write a full-length book for? Consider publishing a Kindle Single instead! Learn more here: <u>How to Submit a Kindle Single</u>

More ideas can be found here: eBook Ideas for Any Niche

Highly Recommended & Insightful Further Reading

- The Economics of Self-Publishing
- 20 Companies That Will Get Your Book Printed
- How to Self-Publish an eBook

THINK:
- Inspiration. What do you know best? Writing what you know is easy when you're an expert in a specific niche or when you are aware of your passions or favorite genres. It's important to be familiar with your strengths as a writer and as a creative individual.

PLAN:
- Lots of content written for your book. Make it the best you possibly can, put your everything into it.

GET:
- If you can afford to hire a professional editor to proofread and edit your manuscript, do it! Otherwise, be prepared to spend some time on doing it yourself. Reach out to those you know for help with this, as they are sure to catch errors you miss and make suggestions to strengthen the the parts of your writing that could use some improvement.

PLAN:
- Write an outline for your book, especially if it's non-fiction. Sometimes writing the outline BEFORE you write the book can be very useful for planning and organizing the content. Use it to streamline the writing process.

GO:
- Search the internet and do some research about self-publishing a novel. Read blogs written by successful writers like J.A. Konrath, they offer a wealth of information to publishing newbies.

Step #2: Prepare and Format Your eBook Files

The formatting of your book is incredibly important and this step is fairly involved, so don't expect to get it done successfully on the first try or in a single day's time.

You will find that different distribution channels require different formats, which can be a real struggle when trying to ensure that your text displays correctly across all devices. This is important and you must test your ebook before making it available to purchase, or risk losing your formatting and having your text appear garbled and mutilated on different reading devices.

The formatting will likely need to be different for each site you use to self-publish your books. What looks great in print may not be readable on a Kindle device, and the same PDF file you upload to Lulu may look awful in your Createspace version.

eBook File Formats

- ePub
- PDF
- HTML
- Mobipocket
- Kindle

The formats listed above are only the most commonly used for creating eBooks, but there are more. For a longer and more detailed list of file formats, visit this Wikipedia link: Comparison of eBook Formats

Most Helpful File Conversion Resources

- If you need to convert your HTML or PDF ebook file to an ePub format, check out this list of tools: Tools to Create ePub eBook Files From PDFs and HTML

- Download the Calibre eBook management software here:http://www.calibre-ebook.com This is a priceless resource for converting eBooks to different file formats. If you need some help learning how to do this, visit this tutorial: How to Convert PDFs to ePub or Kindle Files

- HTML editors can be used to edit ePub files. Learn more here: Edit ePub eBooks With Your Favorite HTML Editor

- Download the OpenOffice word processing software here: http://www.openoffice.org Need help formatting your book layout using OpenOffice? Read this tutorial: Layout a

Book With OpenOffice: Part 1

- [BookGlutton](#) is another tool you can use to convert to ePub.
- [Mobipocket Developer Center](#) is a great resource for creating .Mobi eBook files.
- [eCub](#) is a user-friendly opensource software program that allows you to create both ePub and .Mobi files.
- [Sigil](#) is an opensource WYSIWYG eBook editor that is free to download.To get started using Sigil, check out this helpful tutorial: [Creating ePub eBooks With Sigil](#)
- You can find a very nice collection of professional file conversion services by visiting this directory: [eBook Conversion Service Directory](#)
- [Feedbooks](#) is an online solution that makes it easy to create ePub books.
- [yWriter5](#) is a free novel writing software that you can download for free. This is a great resource for fiction writers, but I found it incredibly helpful when trying to organize my memoir/journal as well.

If you would like some handy copyright samples for your eBook, visit this link: [Copyright Page Samples You Can Copy and Paste Into Your Book](#)

Also, Lulu is a print-on-demand publisher that allows you to publish both eBooks as well as print versions. They have created a free guide for creating eBooks, which can be downloaded here: [eBook Creator Guide](#)

Formatting Trouble

If this is something you've never done before and you have no prior experience formatting eBooks or anything like that, try to relax and stay calm. It's not going to turn out right on your first attempt.

It can get pretty frustrating, some of the steps in the formatting process took me countless tries before I produced satisfactory results.

It's tedious and certainly won't be the most exciting or enjoyable part of self-publishing your eBook, but it's a necessary evil and must be done. Not only must it be done, but it has to be done well or else you can basically expect to sell zero copies.

The Kindle displays text in awful, awful ways when your formatting is lost and a PDF file, for example, is converted using Amazon's upload tool. Ugh! Be sure to preview how it will look, and be prepared for the worst. This is not something you will have ready in a single day, so when you start feeling the urge to yank your hair from your head, it's time to take a much-needed break.

Come back to it in a day or so. Pace yourself. This is supposed to be fun. It's an adventure. It comes with its challenges, but don't be stressed out by them. Just drop it when you need to. Stay positive and determined. I know that if I can figure it out after enough failed attempts, pretty much anyone can do it!

Amazon Publishing Tips

Find more tips, suggestions, information and resources by visiting this lens I created: Self-Publishing on Amazon's Kindle Direct Publishing Platform

GET:
- Your eBook in PDF format.
- Your eBook in HTML format.
- Your eBook in Kindle format.
- Your eBook in ePub format.
- Your eBook in Mobipocket format.

THINK:
- Choose a compelling and relevant title for your eBook. If appropriate, also carefully choose a subtitle that compliments your eBook title.

GET:
- Include a copyright and title page in your eBook files. Also, a table of contents if needed.

PLAN:
- ALWAYS test your eBook files to ensure that your formatting displays properly on each publishing platform you submit it to.

Step #3: Design a High-Quality Cover Art for Your eBook

Whether foolish or not, we all judge books by their covers. Silly as that may be, we do. For this reason, it's imperative that your eBook be sporting an eye-catching and attractive cover design.

If you are serious about giving your story a real chance, do not ignore or neglect the importance of this step.

You have several options when it comes to a cover design for your eBook. The most appropriate choice will be determined mostly by your level of graphic design knowledge/skill and your budget.

Hiring a Freelance Graphic Designer

Do you have somewhere between $300 and $400 to invest in a professional graphic designer for your cover art? If you do, that's certainly your best bet. Take your time searching for the right artist. Be sure to really explore their portfolio until you see the type of art that fits with your book and your story. Do your research and don't rush through this selection process. You'll thank yourself later.

Contact a few artists who offer book cover design services and discuss your project with them, to establish a clear understanding of what your book is about and what type of art would best represent it. Get a feel for their artistic vision and brainstorm ideas with them. Be open to suggestions, but be firm about the elements of your design which you feel strongly about. An experienced artist that's worth your money will be able to balance their talents with your input, and that will be obvious as you continue to work with them.

Don't just immediately go with the first artist who you think can do the job or whose past work impresses you the most. If you're going to spend that kind of money, be choosy and see what more than one has to offer. Ask any questions that you think are important. Find out what is included in their book cover design service. If they offer different packages, ask the questions necessary to determine which best meets your needs.

If you want to check out some graphic designers, but have no idea where to start, try checking out the cover designer that works with self-publishing superstar J.A. Konrath (you may be familiar with his success story). You can find his cover designer's website by visiting this link: http://extendedimagery.blogspot.com His name is Carl Graves and you can trust his service, since he works with one of the most successful self-published authors selling on Amazon. Can't dispute that, right? If his style isn't what you're looking for, just bring up Google and start your search with something like "freelance graphic book cover designer." They should know where to send you.

Another helpful resource for finding freelancers is forums, like the ones offered by KIndle Direct Publishing, CreateSpace and Lulu. There is tons of great talent to be discovered in all of these, just take a peek.

Using a Print-on-Demand Service

Another option you always have is to use one of the print-on-demand or self-publishing services you plan on publishing through. A couple examples are CreateSpace and Lulu, both of which offer professional cover design services. My biggest problem with graphic design services offered by big sites like these is the huge difference in price.

If you would rather not spend the time searching for a freelance artist and money is not an issue, this may be worth considering. Just be prepared to spend significantly more than most freelancers will charge to end up with a decent cover design package from a site like these. Pay close attention to how many revisions are included in the pricing package you are interested in.

For example, Lulu offers three different pricing packages for professional cover design services. The first is their "Basic" design service, which in my opinion is far too basic to be worth paying for. The other two are the only ones likely to be of a high enough quality that I could recommend paying for.

However, I'm reluctant to suggest their "Premium" or "Custom" design packages to anyone, unless money is not at all a concern and your budget is generous, to say the least. Premium covers from Lulu run at $450 a pop, while a truly customized design is priced at just under $1,000. Sheesh.

Similarly, CreateSpace offers book cover design services that start at just $99 and run as high as Lulu's Custom package, though they have several more pricing options between the two extremes. If I had to guess, that translates to varying degrees of mediocrity rather than a wider variety of high-quality options worth your money. I could be wrong though. That's just the way it looks, as I'm checking each one out right now.

Graphic Design on a Shoestring Budget

Okay, I saved this option for now since it is both last and certainly least. In monetary terms, at least. For authors or aspiring writers who just don't have lumps of cash to throw around like some others may, there are a couple of rather cheap and creative ideas to explore that can actually leave you with some acceptable or even impressive results.

Yep, it's true. You can cut some corners here, if you're willing. The nice thing about trying these cheaper and alternative methods is that the investment is small enough that it's well worth the risk you take.

That means if you don't like what you get, it won't mean spending hundreds of dollars on your second attempt at the right cover design for your book. That sounds very good to me, which is one of the reasons I went this route.

The other reason was that I had a budget of about, oh, nothing. At least to start. Once I got my first months payments from my Amazon Kindle sales, I was able to invest some of that money in promoting my eBook and upgrading some of my book's other elements also.

I had tons of fun with that, so you definitely can to. I am hoping that this will help you do just that --- have a lot of fun doing something new that you haven't tried before and even finding out you can be successful and make some extra monthly income in the process. Can't beat that.

All right, so if you need some graphic design on the super cheap...there are two main things you can consider or give a try.

The first is to see what kind of quality you are able to find on a site like Fiverr. In case you're not familiar with Fiverr, it's a neat site where people can post the things they are willing to do in exchange for a flat rate of $5.

You may be thinking, who gets a professional eBook cover design for only $5? That's impossible! Well, that may be half way true. But it might not be. I'll let you decide on your own, based on the experience I had using the site.

So I did a quick search for eBook cover design and saved a good handful of "gigs" that looked appealing or possibly worth looking into further. After I had a good sampling, I contacted a couple of the sellers and we started chatting back and forth about my book cover and the type of design I was envisioning.

Here is a priceless tip for using Fiverr. If you want to get better work than what $5 will buy, simply offer to order their gig multiple times. So, when I had chosen an artist that I was ready to buy from I offered to order the gig three times if I was really happy with the design, but committed to a minimum of twice to ensure that she would be paid $10, rather than only $5. Not a huge difference, but I was playing around and wanted to see how it would turn out.

After coming to an agreement and explaining in as much detail as I could how I wanted the cover to look, she went to work. She got back to me when she was done, which was very fast. I was pleasantly surprised with the results. Ordered the third time to show my appreciation and offer it as a tip for her help.

It was far from what $400 will get you, but it looked good enough that I felt it was acceptable to use as my initial Kindle eBook cover design. You can check out the cover design here: http://db.tt/fzVvhGft Not too shabby for the price, eh?

Learning Photoshop or GIMP

This one is only for people who are not in any rush to get their eBook self-published. If this is mostly something you are having fun with and doing at your leisure, then you may want to consider giving this a try, just to find out if it's even something you would be interested in enough to explore.

We all know that Photoshop is a spendy piece of software and is really designed for serious graphic artists who understand advanced techniques that you will probably have no idea how to dabble with as a beginner.

I suggest downloading an opensource alternative called GIMP, which can do essentially all the neat stuff that can be accomplished using Photoshop and is 100% free. You can find the download by visiting their official site at the following address: http://www.gimp.org

If you've never tried to create any sort of computer graphic before (like in my case) then you should probably head straight over to YouTube, which will be your best friend if you want to take a stab at designing a decent cover art for your eBook from scratch. I have always been intrigued in creating computer graphics, just never had a good enough reason to start teaching myself until I needed a book cover.

So I watched some tutorials on how to create a book cover design using GIMP, though I was somewhat disappointed with the selection and quality of the available tutorials. I've still not been able to find one that does a good job of showing you how to create a Kindle optimized cover design for an ebook.

What I as able to find was several that helped me learn the basics and figure out how to kind of experiment on my own until I came up with something halfway acceptable.

My results? Using the Lulu cover templates, I created this design for my print book: http://dl.dropbox.com/u/12622552/cover.png Far from perfect, but not awful considering I had no clue what I was doing at all. Just watched a couple of YouTube videos (that got paused every few seconds for over an hour, lol!)

PLAN:
- A realistic budget for your cover design. Choose which of the following ranges is most realistic for you: $50-$100, $300-$400 or $500+

- If going with a professional service from a print-on-demand company, be sure you understand what is included in each pricing package and contact their team to figure out which one makes the most sense for your book/project

- If you decide to hire a freelance graphic designer, spend some time searching and exploring all the online talent. Ask lots of questions, find the right artist for your book.

- Every book needs a good title. Make it descriptive, powerful and one to remember. Pick one that best conveys the overall message of or theme of your book. Put some thought into it. Be sure no one has used it already.

- Before you start discussing your cover design project with any artists, do your best to create a mental image of what you would like or what you have in mind as a cover design. Pick your preferred fonts for the title, author name, subtitle, etc. Choose your desired color scheme. Have both of these ready when you contact an artist.

GET:
- Quotes from more than one graphic artist whose portfolio seems to fit with the type of art you like best.

- Your cover design artwork optimized for each individual distribution channel that you will upload your eBook to. Make sure to get the dimensions correct for proper display, particularly on Amazon (since they automatically resize your image to display in different sizes).

GO:
- To create your own cover design for a Lulu print book, select the appropriate book size from their templates found here: Lulu Book Specs

- To download the correct size cover template for your Createspace paperback, visit this link: Createspace Cover Specs

THINK:
- No matter what route you decide to go, always find out how many revisions are included with the cover design service you are going to purchase. Don't get stuck with the first design, even if you are unhappy with it. Be sure they include at least a couple of revisions before you spend a significant amount of money.

Step #4: Upload eBook to Sales Distribution Channels & Set Price

Once your eBook files are all created, polished, converted and up to standards, it's time to go ahead and take the biggest, scariest step that you're going to take when self-publishing your story. That's right. It's time to submit it to sites like Amazon, Barnes & Noble, Smashwords, Lulu and tons of others, if you so desire.

Print-on-Demand Companies

If you would like to produce a print version of your book, I highly suggest Lulu over other print-on-demand services. They are a tad bit more expensive than some competitors, but I must say that the quality of their books is worth the difference in price. At least in my opinion.

If you are considering a print-on-demand service such as CreateSpace, I will simply warn you that their proof/review copies are far less likely to turn out correct than Lulu, at least in my own experience.

I still haven't made my own book available on CreateSpace (which is useful, because it makes your book available in both print and digitally for Amazon customers) due to several review copies which butchered the interior formatting.

The results from Lulu turned out perfectly on the first go, and their process was far more user-friendly. Another thing that I liked about using Lulu for print copies was they do not require you to order a proof/review copy to evaluate before making your print book available for sale.

Using their book creation tool, you are able to view the interior and the cover EXACTLY how it will look in print. This saves you both money and time in getting your book for sale in print, without risking improper or messed up formatting. Much better option, at least for me.

The biggest drawback is that you can't expect as many sales through Lulu as CreateSpace likely can offer. But if you want to order some physical copies of your book to give away, sell or whatever else, Lulu is the best bet.

Obtaining an ISBN for Each Print and Digital Edition of Your Book

You will need to obtain separate ISBNs for each print and digital edition of your book/eBook. You have two options when it comes to this. You can shell out the cash to buy your own ISBN from a site such as this: http://www.isbn.org/standards/home/index.asp for around $125 (for one ISBN) or you can opt to be assigned a free ISBN through the publishing distribution channel you are using to make your book available for sale.

Lulu, Createspace and B&N all offer free ISBNs for self-published books and eBooks. As far as I am aware, there is no disadvantage to choosing a free ISBN, rather than buying one. I went with free, and that has worked fine for me.

Amazon Kindle eBooks do not require an ISBN. Instead, Amazon assigns each eBook in the Kindle store with an ASIN instead. That stands for "Amazon Standard Identification Number" and is a unique number associated with your eBook and used to identify your product across the site. This number is the last part of your Amazon product page URL.

For example, my eBook product page can be found at the following address: http://www.amazon.com/dp/B004C446IC and my ASIN is the *B004C446IC* portion of the URL.

The absence of an ISBN for your Kindle version is kind of a drawback, in my opinion. While it does not at all affect your ability to sell eBooks on Amazon, there are lots of other sites (such as review sites, and other places to list your book) that do require an ISBN.

What this means is that you will need to get a free ISBN from one of the other sites in order to list your book on these sites, since Amazon Kindle does not require or assign one. That's fairly easy to do, however. No major thing there.

Of course, if you are planning on primarily selling your eBook on Amazon or just want to start with that, you don't need to worry so much about having an ISBN for the moment.

Pricing Your eBook

Obviously you have sorted out most of the little details for your eBook prior to this step in the self-publishing process.

You have chosen a descriptive, suitable title that you believe best conveys the story told in your book. You've obtained a professional looking cover design to represent it visually to potential customers and readers. You have your interior files all properly converted and optimized to ensure proper formatting across all file types and devices that people will be reading your work on.

There is only one small but very important detail left to decide. That, of course, is how much you are going to charge for your eBook.

This one requires a bit of thought and demands that you take a few different factors into consideration. Only you can make the final call on this, so don't put too much weight into the advice you read in blogs, articles and other places you discover online. eBooks are a fairly new landscape for entrepreneurs and no one will suggest anything that is golden and guaranteed to work for all authors.

The best thing about this decision is that you are able to change it at any time and by any amount you wish. If your initial price isn't selling or you have second thoughts (believe you may have under priced or overpriced it, after giving it more thought) all you have to do is edit the number you originally entered as the price. It's quite easy. That simple.

An Important Note on Changing Prices

If you do decide to change the price of your eBook in the future, you need to be sure of one thing. Always edit the price on ALL sites where you are selling your eBook, so that you are charging the same amount for the eBook on all sites where it is available.

DO NOT price your eBook on Amazon for $10.00 and forget to update the price on Barnes & Noble, where customers can still purchase it for $5.99. This is very important.

Don't look unprofessional or upset any of the distribution channels you are using by offering the same product at a lower price on a competitor's site.

Experimenting With Different Prices

Other than making sure your prices are consistent across all sales channels, feel free to experiment with different amounts and see what kind of results you get. As a general rule, most sites will advise unknown and first-time authors to price their work on the lower end initially. This is common sense advice and probably sensible to start with.

A traditionally published friend of mine suggested that I bump up the price of my eBook from the original $1.99 to $4.99 after the first four months it was available for sale. He explained that such a price increase was reasonable and justified now that I'd gotten my foot in the door, so to speak.

Not having any experience with publishing before this, I decided to take his advice as an experienced author. To my surprise, the increase in price did not affect my overall monthly profits. I sold slightly fewer copies, but made quite a bit more per sale. It ended up all coming out close to the same for me, which was good.

So don't limit yourself where price is concerned. Just give each new price a fair trial period before changing it again or drawing any big conclusions. All you need to keep in mind is that no digital price tag is set in stone! Find the price that works best for your and maximizes your profits and go with whatever that is.

For a more detailed tutorial that includes annotated screen shots, please check out my Amazon Kindle Direct Publishing how-to article found here: Written an eBook? Start Selling it on Amazon Today!

This tutorial will walk you through each step of uploading your files to Amazon's Kindle Store and is great for beginners and anyone who is new to the process.

Not in the Mood to Read?

Then try checking out these 5 awesome slideshare presentations that offer quick, visually engaging but highly useful information about self-publishing and the whole process: 5 Great Slideshare Presentations on eBook Publishing

Think You're Ready?

I've created this checklist for you to review before moving on: Self-Publishing Checklist

GO:
- Sign up for Kindle Direct Publishing and upload your finished Kindle version to the site, using
- Next, head on over to Barnes & Noble's "PubIt" and repeat a similar process of uploading your PDF or other eBook file.
- Last stop is Lulu, if you'd like a print version of your book. Use their simple and relatively easy creator to format and design your book, display and review your files once uploaded, choose the right book size, finalize your book and order your first physical copy!

THINK:
- Consider the countless other print-on-demand and eBook publishing sites you can sell your book through, such as Smashwords, CreateSpace and many others. Expect fewer sales than Amazon has to offer, though some are still worth checking out.

PLAN:
- Once you've uploaded your eBook files to Kindle Direct Publishing, expect to wait somewhere between 1-2 business days while they catalog, index and prepare your product page. Once this process is complete, your eBook will be available for purchase and you should be in business!

GET:
- An ISBN for each digital and print edition of your book.

Step #5: Effectively Market & Promote Your eBook

I'm going to be brutally honest with you. This step is actually more important than any of the other ones, at least by themselves. Yes, that's correct.

But how can marketing and promoting your eBook be more important than creating the book to begin with?!

Because all the work that you will put into creating your eBook will bring you almost no results without effective marketing and eBook promotion. I promise that. It's a bummer for a lot of writers when they hear it.

Lots of authors do not consider themselves marketers or sales types. The good news is that you certainly don't have to be. I know I'm not either. I'm a writer. That's what I do. I'm not into selling things.

See, marketing and promoting your book is very different than trying to push sales. You may associate the two, but they are totally independent of each other and fundamentally different games altogether. Trust me here. I figured this all out as I went. I didn't know the first thing about marketing, promotion and had no clue about sales when I started out on this little venture.

Luckily, as an author you will be far more involved and active in terms of publicity and branding than anything directly related to the aforementioned scarier sounding areas of expertise which have reputations for being dreadfully boring in comparison.

Let's go into greater detail now and figure out how to execute the marketing and promotional plans that are forming as we speak and read.

eBook Reviews

A great and easy place to start is getting reviews for your eBook from fans, readers and even reviewers/bloggers. The easiest and most effortless way to start getting reader reviews unsolicited is simply by waiting for them to show up on your Amazon Kindle product page, which will happen. It can take some time, but you can count on a few popping up once you've sold a few copies.

Now, for a bit of slightly bad news: good luck getting any newspaper reviewers or big review sites to even consider your self-published eBook. Fat friggin' chance. Just save yourself the time and don't bother.

But! Don't be too discouraged. As the self-published revolution continues to gain popularity, there are some great new review sites and online efforts being formed and some of them are definitely worth checking out.

My Top Picks for Review Sites

- The highly coveted Midwest Book Review.
    - **Pros:** highly reputable and places priority on independently published books.
    - **Cons:** only accepts physical copies and requires two in order to be considered for review. Does not guarantee review.
- IndieReader
    - A newer but promising review site for self-published titles that already features lots of insightful eBook reviews. Worth checking out for sure.
- ReadersFavorite
    - Older review site that has a good reputation and allows you to submit your eBook using their submission form. Does not guarantee a review, but will notify you by email if and when your book is reviewed. I managed to score with this site.
- ManicReaders
    - Neat social type site for authors that allows you to upload a copy of your eBook for review and offers a "review depot" that includes over a dozen review sites that you can submit your title to. No guarantee for review, but I managed to snag a review from the site!
- LLBookReview
    - Nice blog-style review site with several regular book reviewers. Willing to accept eBooks and has good reputation for independent book reviews for several years. Must email reviewers to pitch them for review, I was able to capture the interest of Shannon Yarbrough, who was kind enough to review my eBook.
- Literary R&R
    - A nice book review blog maintained by a friendly avid reader named Mandy. Contacted via email and she agreed to review my eBook!

For more help on approaching bloggers to review your book, read my blog post by visiting this link: Pitching Book Bloggers to Review Your eBook - Best Practices

Want to give away free review copies of your eBook to book bloggers? Find out how here: How to Give Away Free Review Copies

Radio, Blog & Podcast Interviews

Landing opportunities for radio, blog or podcast interviews can be a great form of free author publicity and are essential in the online branding process. While interviews don't always necessarily have a direct relationship to increased book sales, they do help you more as an author over the long term.

That is, if you do a few important things. First of all, ALWAYS politely request an MP3 copy of all your interviews before your interview date. Show producers and hosts are very willing to accommodate you, but in the event that they are unable to do this, you can find free tools online that will let you record them yourself.

Not sure where or how to find interview opportunities? Yeah, neither was I. I didn't have the first clue, actually. So tons of research and a handful of successful interviews (radio, blog and podcast) later, I have discovered that it's easy as pie.

My Top Picks for Author Interview Opportunities

- RadioGuestList
  - This is a cool site that will let you sign up for email or RSS notifications to alert you whenever a radio or podcast show host or producer posts a request for guests on their show. Just read the descriptions they provide to make sure you are the right type of guest they are seeking. They are usually looking for a specific demographic that somehow relates to the theme of their show, so make sure the pitches you send make sense and are appropriate. Try not to waste your time or theirs and always be polite and respectful. I've landed several interviews through this site.
- ArtistFirst Radio Network
  - This site has a weekly show called "Author's First" which is an hour-long interview with an independent author. You can book your show for a minimum donation of only $10. They were friendly, plugged my book and overall was a good experience.

Press Release Distribution

If you're a writer or an author, then writing your own press release shouldn't be too difficult for you once you understand how they need to be written and formatted. Don't worry, it's pretty simple and I wrote my own press release to announce the publication of my eBook after a bit of research.

I'd never written one before that either. This is a cake walk. For specific instructions that guide you through the process and clearly explain the whole idea, read my blog post here: How to Write a Quality Press Release

Now it's time to choose distribution channels for your press release. There are tons of free sites that rank well. Find a good list I put together by visiting this link: Free and Paid Press Release Distribution Services

I highly recommend considering an affordable paid distribution package from PRWeb if you can make a small and reasonable investment to promote your eBook.

I purchased their $140 standard package and was delighted with the awesome results I received from media contacts, activists related to my writing and was very impressed with the detailed stats and analytics provided for a full four weeks after your release goes live.

For an example, you can see my own eBook press release here: My Press Release

PRWeb's paid distribution landed me my first radio interview on a Canadian rock station. It also resulted in an invitation to do a live reading in New York City at a monthly event held by an activist who fights for sex worker rights (I am a sex worker, and wrote a memoir).

I was also contacted by the producer for a nationally syndicated radio show called "Your Time With Kim Iverson" and was asked for an interview, which I accepted. Best $140 I have spent in a long time. Great customer support!

PLAN:
- A brief, effective email pitch that introduces you and provides a snapshot of what your book is about. Send it to bloggers who write book reviews, after carefully reviewing their submission policies to make sure your genre is accepted

- Customize an email pitch that is targeted at radio and podcast shows seeking author and expert guests. Send it out to hosts and producers who request guests like yourself

- Write a press release to announce your eBook publication and generate some buzz surrounding your book. Capture the interest of the public as well as reporters and media contacts.

GET:
- Reader reviews from fans on Amazon, friends, family and anyone else you can encourage to give you feedback

- Choose a free or paid (or both) press release distribution service and send out your release when it's ready

- Always ask (politely, of course) for an MP3 copy of your interview before your scheduled date, so you can host the file on your own website after the interview airs

THINK:
- Always have proper etiquette and manners as a guest on a show. Don't forget to say thank you to the host and refer to them by name during your interview. Be on time. Avoid background noise for phone interviews.

GO:
- Visit my blog for more book marketing and promotion tips: eBook Marketing Tips for Self-Published Authors

Step #6: Social Media Presence & Author Branding

Okay, so social media is nothing new. We've all heard plenty about it and how great it can be to build your online presence. Well, it works great for authors too. It's especially helpful for communicating with your readers, building a loyal fan base and engaging with your audience in a variety of ways.

First stop is Twitter. Second stop is Facebook. Third stop is LinkedIn. Make sure you are on all three.

Find eBook readers on LinkedIn here: 5 LinkedIn Groups for eBook Readers

Your ultimate goal when using social media will be to build an "author platform." You may have heard this term before, but it encompasses many different elements and describes a very wide range of tools you should be using to your advantage.

Social Sites for Authors

- GoodReads
    - This site is a must-have for all authors and aspiring writers alike. If you aren't already on the site, you must go register now. This resource is invaluable. There are so many neat things you can do. Start by creating an author profile, list your eBooks/books next. Then, add some of your quotes if you want. Start a discussion group. Make friends. Ask for reviews. You can even upload your eBook to sell on the site if you'd like. The best way to use GoodReads to promote your books is to hold a free book giveaway contest. This is only available for print books, but it's worth doing. Order a few copies from Lulu and start a giveaway. GoodReads will pick the winners, somewhat based on who is likely to be interested in your type of book or genre. This is an outstanding and reliable way to get some thoughtful book reviews on the site, from avid readers. You are responsible for shipping the books to the winners.
- ManicReaders
    - We mentioned this site for their cool review depot, but it is also a great social reader and writer community as well. Explore what it has to offer and create an author profile!
- Author's Den
    - This site is similar to the previous two mentioned. Create an author profile, upload some of your work. Play around with the features and check out the possibilities offered by this social author site.
- Amazon Author's Central
    - This is a great service provided by Amazon. Once you register your profile, it will appear towards the bottom of your eBook's product page. People can click on it and it will take them to a profile where you can add an RSS feed to your blog,

upload author photos, submit an author bio and also allows you to track your sales and recent customer reviews, when you log in. Must-have for anyone selling their book on Amazon.

New, Innovative Social Author Resources

- BookWhirl
  - This is a free (with paid options as well) promotional site for authors that allows them to create a listing for their titles and generate a neat author widget with a preview of their work.
- Storify
  - A very neat and brand new app for building and creating stories centered around a topic or person using social media search engines. Easy drag-and-drop interface allows you to add content from Twitter, YouTube, etc. Do a search for your book title and add search results to your "story." Fun to play with.
- Kindlegraph
  - Very cool way to add autographs/signatures to your eBooks for fans and readers who collect autographed copies. Easy sign in with Twitter account and other users can request a signed copy.
- NovelRank
  - Incredibly useful app that will generate an RSS feed to update every time you sell a copy of your eBook on Amazon. Great sales tracking tool and totally free to use.
- Odyl
  - A new app for promoting your books on Facebook.
- Zinepal
  - Really great way to turn your blog into an eBook. Customize it, add advertisements and other images, etc. Only $5 per ebook with custom options, or you can buy a monthly subscription.

More Promotional Ideas

- **Start a newsletter** for your readers, fans and social media followers.

  Use a service like Tiny Letter to get started with a simple newsletter to keep your audience up to speed with your latest activity.

- MatchPoint. This is a paid service, but they offer a free ten day trial. Copy and paste your press release into their media kit setup and fill out all the additional fields.

  Use their awesome search engine to plug a few relevant tags (that have to do with your book and/or writing) and search for bloggers and journalists who have covered those topics recently. Then, you can jot down a quick and personalized pitch to each one you want to contact individually and send them your press kit at the same time. Track how many of them open and view your message and other materials.

I was able to connect with a journalist for my local newspaper, the Oregonian by using this great resource. I was interviewed and managed to get my column featured on the front page of the section my story was featured in. Priceless!

- **Article marketing** and user-generated content sites.

    Start with eZineArticles or Squidoo. Create content that relates to the type of writing you do. Promote your books by including "spotlight Amazon reviews" in your Squidoo lenses. Drive sales.

Great Blogs for Further Reading

- Self-Publishing Review
- Newbie's Guide to Self-Publishing
- GalleyCat
- The Book Designer
- Self-Publishing Team
- Password Incorrect Blog
- Book Marketing Maven

PLAN:
- Hold a free book giveaway contest on GoodReads. I recommend listing 3 books for your first giveaway. You must ship books to winners, print books only.

- Optimize your Amazon product page. Select appropriate categories when uploading your eBook. Ask others to add relevant tags to your eBook. Sign-up for Author Central and complete your profile.

- Use sites like Twitter to hold book giveaway contests and offer other freebies and prizes to your followers

- Be easy to contact and get in touch with. Be sure your press release contains accurate, updated contact info (phone, email, social media, etc.) and be available to answer calls from media outlets and other persons of interest.

- Do your best to be professional and build relationships with everyone you come in contact with as an author. That includes journalists, activists, organizations, readers, fans, followers, enthusiasts, other authors and writers, show hosts, producers, absolutely everyone!

GET:
- Signed up on Twitter, Facebook and LinkedIn. Update regularly and find out who is talking about you and your book on all of these sites. Join in the conversation. Respond to your readers and fans.

- Be everywhere. When someone learns about you or your writing, the first thing they will do is google you. Make sure the results are many and great.

- Your own domain and website. Start an author blog. Promote your writing there too. Turn your blog into an eBook and offer it as a freebie or a bonus with other products.

- A free newsletter subscription service up and running, so your followers and fans can register to receive updates and news about what you are up to and your latest work.

THINK:
- Brainstorm new and creative ways to use existing social media apps and other online resources to connect with your audience and promote your writing

My name is Ashly Lorenzana. I am a freelance writer, blogger and self-published author of a memoir titled "Sex, Drugs & Being an Escort," which was originally a personal journal I wrote in occasionally during the five years I spent working as an escort in Portland, OR.

If you'd like to read more about self-publishing for Kindle and other platforms, please visit my publishing blog where I am always adding new tips for author marketing and eBook promotion.

I hope you've enjoyed this self-publishing primer and best of luck to you in all your writing adventures!

www.ingramcontent.com/pod-product-compliance
Lightning Source LLC
LaVergne TN
LVHW020508080526
838202LV00057B/6231